The Dance Of The Poltergeists

the flow of unfulfilled dreams and
unfounded fears

RITU GUPTA

Made with ♥ on the BookLeaf Publishing Platform
www.bookleafpub.in
www.bookleafpub.com

Dedication

Words - and how they hold space for my broken
emotions and kiss my cracked dry deserts of cheeks with
their moistness, saltness, sweetness
how the nip of the pen acupunctures my heart to flow
out all what it holds
how they acupressurize my heart to revive and start
feeling the febrility of life
how these imperfect realities of my life are held perfectly
by words in their ingenious scaffolding
how this army of words immortalizes the mortal
moments
how the things that life doesn't not want, are wanted in
poems
this universe of words, words that are the limbs of my
soul

Preface

there is this acute awareness in me, a resounding
resonance that
the only way for me to exist is to write
and that is my glimmer against any trigger

Acknowledgements

Shaurya- who knows my truth more than I know it
Piyush - who makes life worth living every single day.
He is my home.
Shirdi Sai Baba - who has taken me from human
consciousness to Sai consciousness,
a place where I learnt the contrapunt of life - it is in
surrender, one finds true empowerment.

. of buttons and mountains

I am more intrigued by the
flatness of a button
than by the height of a mountain
try saying
a girl on the mountain
a girl with a button
which evokes more mystery?
after all you can find a deep indigo button
but you can't find a deep indigo mountain
and then you can lose a button
but you can't lose a mountain
and then during spring cleaning
you will find your lost button
but you can't find a mountain
isn't it such fun
to talk of a button and compare it with a mountain

# of Treetment

I wish I could hang upside down
on life
like some of the branches
of the trees
that go down
are they humbler than the ones going up
the heavier they are
the more down they go
towards earth
towards roots
pulled by the gravitational force of the earth
does that mean gravitas
that the more you are grounded
the more gravitas you have
these thoughts dance like poltergeists in my mind
alive
yet going down
more I grow
the more I bend

tabula rasa

memories
are ghosts
they come out in the night
they belong to us
yet so alien
so distant
so inaccessible
they have my own people
our very own
but now they don't listen to us
they don't come
they just make me long, long, long for them. .
my people
they don't listen to me
I go and look for them behind the curtains
on the chair
in the foyer
they are not there
but they are in my memories
they are Becoming sepia in my mind --

memories are ghosts--they suddenly arise in our
consciousness and then we feel possessed
I can never experience tabula-rasa

fenestrations

the rules
that I make for myself
are my own fenestrations
they give me the best
combination of world
inside them
and beyond them and they never let me fall
by bending too much
rules we make are
our own intentionality

solitary is my soul-tree

solitary
I become my soul-tree
I hug myself
and I breathe the scent of my soul
and I drop all the dry twigs
all that has lived its course
it is so transformative
it is so rejuvenating

After

how does it feel to be dead
last night
I lived many lives
in search of joy
in search of meaning
I thought of all my relations
but they all are transactional
emotional
ambivalent ones
I am not needed in my own life
I will go and they will go to -
to work
to sleep
to sky
to sea deep
they will be asked to move on
they will
they will dehumanise me
will call me soul
as if they have seen

oh you still don't see your end
that's what
you will make a death -cafe
to experience death
no one can experience death
not those who are alive
because they are not dead yet
and nor those who are dead
because they are dead
so how do we know what death is
and we are solving the big conundrums.
for me death is
when an emotion is killed that it can never rise again

# of puppets and puppeteers

the puppet
is the subject
of the will of the puppeteer
but puppeteer is nothing without
its puppets
so where is the agency vested ?

can I see who mourns my death

and if there would be an AI
For the 'dead me' to see
who mourns my death
and how much my people miss me

do they become deilrious
do they not want to be
how long they go hungry
do they laugh
do they watch movies
do they still believe in life

will my child find anyone as loving as me
will my husband find a new She
but my mother will not find another daughter
mother will keep this space empty

Sun-she

if sun would be a She
how would it be
if sun would be a She
there would be no patriarchy

phantom pain

those pains
that come from distance
which is so close
the ones that come from
the absence
that is so present

senior moment

and then I forgot
who I was
and what I did
and where I was going
it was not alzheimers
it was absence of thoughts
and I would call it
senior moment
or spiritual moment.

Veja du

between the mundane
and the miraculous
you exist
for whatever mundanity we live together
or whatever miracles we both witness and experience
there are moments when you , very you, very very you
look to me
so new , so new , so new
veje du
veja du.

Duende

to do or not to do
I should do
as what is the harm to have few
I should not do
as I already have quite a few
this quite a few and few
to do or not to do
am I manifesting
chasing
aspiring
or craving
pining
or yearning
are they all the same
do we get this clarity ever
is life a math
for math is its a philosophy
its all a mixed pot
I am my own duende

Liminal

I am a liminality
between
two thoughts
I am the stairway
the elevator
between two spaces
between two souls
between two goals
I am the pathway
the segue
I am a punching bag
a rheostat
a ritual
my existence is of connecting
a waiting room for emotional and metaphorical changes

eudemonia

a guava
in its perfect colour
and texture
and accessibility
can give me my most eudemonic momen
for I barely yearn for a guava
there are already good things to eat
and in fact most of the times
I don't remember guavas.
and only time I feel a yearning
is when I see them on carts while passing by a highway
but then I don't want to stop the car
and wait
so I forget
for I love guavas but not so much that I will stop my car
and buy
but when I see it perched on my kitchen top
it gives me eudemonic feeling

kenopsia

there lie some ten pens
and some staple pins
a note pad
a long rod
some old photographs
which have become " more old" sic
toothy smiles of people in the photogrpahs
the bucolic innocence
which looks like an innocence now
but that time they thought they are the wisest
but unsuspecting
trusting life to the core
trusting their own steps
trusting the concept of mortality
and there is one transcendencce
a layer of dust
only she was not there
and he was not there
they meant the whole home
and now their absence is so noisy

in its silence
that kenopsia

Funereal

she was alive
she had fun
she was real
but her heart was funereal
innumerable dreams
hopes
aspirations
lay dead there
she carried a grave in her heart
but her heart beat was robust
for she kept the grave alive
may be still in dreams
these dead would wake up
and do a dance of the joylessness
but dance nevertheless

sarees

I opened my wardrobe
and my heart went into a throb
there they all hung in a row
like a gorgeous rainbow
an album of woven memories
my precious possessions Called sarees
we had a silent conversation
with each I have a special relation
my eyes fell on my red patella
I caressed it and it said voila
remember our first day out
you looked a million dollar without doubt
we both looked made for each other
you took care of me like a mother
second was my mustard upadi
I reached out and it smelt Hyderabadi
I said I found you by serendipity
in the whole heap you looked the most pretty
yes it whispered why were you so choosy
you were selecting as if adopting baby

then I looked at my purple paithani
filled with peacocks and raja rani
you are getting into designer ones
take me out at least once
old is gold
it said just hold me
behold me
and then the latest kunbi
bought from a revivalist in Panaji
it sai to me
I have yet to become yours only
till your perfume suffuses me
I am just not your saree
I am waiting when I will be you
and you will be me
and then whispers that were slow
turn into a rising crescendo
we want to go to a party
why are you so melancholy
my eyes well up
and together I hug them and I whisper
to them
there is a lockdown
in the town
all I wear is a gown
I am unkempt
unkept

this is not the time for vanity
any indulgence is inanity
right now trying to survive as human
waiting for the day, when I will have the privilege to be
a woman
then I will take you all out
one by one
in gay abandon
till then, we wait for good times to come

new toppings

and I am told that they
are going for tomato peels
as a topping on the pizza
and then they are putting fruits on pizza
then will pizza still remain a pizza
when will pizza will not look like pizza
because we have so many unpizza pizza
and this thought came to me when I was in ibiza

the irony of deep love

The deep love is protective but possessive.
it appears about each other, but it sometimes is about
Self.
I can't do without you.
I don't know what I would do without you.
I am what I am because of you .
What will I do without you.
think how much of I Is in deep love.
deep love is also a result of deep love for self.

sui-generis

She was life's unique kiss
on the cheeks of this big universe
she was sui-generis

she had no wings
but she hopped like a butterfly miss
she was sui-generis

a bitch goddess
a glorious mess
she was sui-generis

she was neither that
nor was she this
she was sui- generis

she was anyone's wish
she was known to be a bliss

she was sui -generis

she was demotic
she was divine
she was demiurgic
she was swish
she was sui-generis

9 789369 547517